A Handbook for Special N̶e̶e̶d̶s̶

Dedication

This book is dedicated to my mother,
Peggy Cutrupi, who was my inspiration.

Foreword

This book could not have happened without the efforts of many people. They shared their time, their expertise and their support. They are all passionate about improving the lives of others and gladly gave their support to this book.

Those who have traveled with me hold a special place in my heart. We have had many laughs and tears in our travels and made memories that will last forever. I look forward to making many more with you—my new friends.

Special thanks to:

Jerry Shapiro, my editor
Fredi White, FW Graphic Design Group
Angela and Michael Smith, Kessler Research Foundation
Mathew Casteluccio, Helen Hayes Hospital
Elissa Goldstein, Adler Aphasia Center
Linda Winfield, RN, MPH, Columbia University Medical Center
Anthony Cutrupi, just because

❧ Introduction ❧

The purpose of this book is very simple: to help make people with special needs aware of just how much the travel industry changed and how much is being done to make travel for you as easy and stress-free as possible. And to make you aware of just how many special services and organizations are available to meet your needs.

Why is the travel industry doing all this? In some cases, they are complying with government regulations. But more importantly, they recognize an opportunity when they see one. According to the National Center for Health Statistics, over 49 million Americans are living with a disability. That makes you part of a huge, growing and largely untapped market.

It is our goal to provide you with a plan of action to make your dream trip happen. The book is full of tips, tricks and information to make your journey as smooth as possible. But you hold the key to your own success, because the key to every successful trip is careful planning.

Every detail of the trip must be considered and examined and planned for in advance. And every detail needs to be checked and re-checked. This book will help you anticipate and plan for any roadblocks your may face.

Because conditions, accommodations and rules are always changing, it's important for you to have an advocate by your side to help you plan your trip. And the best helpmate you can have on your side is a travel professional that specializes in special needs travel. A person who's been there, who knows the ropes and can help you plan and cut through any barriers. A travel professional who can anticipate your travel needs and help you prepare for any complications that may arise.

Of course, even in today's more positive travel climate, not every vacation is accessible to every special needs traveler. Your travel professional can help you select the most appropriate vacation—the most accessible destinations and the best ways to get there. Work with him/her to find one that is just right for you. You can avoid disappointment by being honest with your travel professional and really taking the time to review all of your wishes and your concerns.

Today it is possible for families to spend time together fully enjoying the wonders of travel, while accommodating each member's travel needs. Multi-generational travel is more popular than ever and is the perfect way for each generation to enjoy and appreciate each other.

The memories you can make are priceless!

This book is organized by specific disability to make it easier for our readers to find the information they need to maximize their travel experience. We will look at a variety of special needs and provide you with ways to deal with the specific issues you may face.

General topics such as travel insurance, air travel, and train and bus travel will be covered separately. No matter what the special needs, there are certain issues that everyone has to deal with.

Travel insurance is a key component of any successful trip. It is especially important for special needs travelers to be properly covered so that you can travel with one less concern. As prepared as your may be, the unexpected can always happen. And travel insurance is one way to deal with some of those unexpected issues and events.

The travel industry is making great strides to deal with all types of special needs. It is much better now than even five years ago, and it's getting better all the time.

This is all in your favor. Take advantage of every new opportunity you can. You do not want to sit home and now you do not have to.

Hopefully, this book will show you that YOU CAN TRAVEL.
So decide what you would like to discover in this fascinating world
we all live in–AND START PLANNING!

Linda C. Cutrupi
linda@mainlyspecialneedstravel.com
www.mainlyspecialneedstravel.com

ᎦᏫ Table of Contents ᎧᏬ

☙ A HANDBOOK ❧
FOR SPECIAL NEEDS TRAVELERS
Linda C. Cutrupi

A Handbook for Special Needs Travelers

WHAT ARE THE BEST ACCESSIBLE VACATIONS?

Whenever I am out speaking to groups, someone always asks me what the best accessible vacation is. In actuality you can have an accessible vacation just about anywhere in the world, from the Galápagos Islands to an accessible African Safari. However, certain locations and types of vacations are very easy and accessible friendly. These are the types of vacations we will be discussing in this article.

CRUISING

By far the easiest vacation is a cruise. And this is true for almost any situation, from early onset Alzheimers to wheelchair travel. Cruises are relaxing, non-stressful, and you only have to unpack once to see multiple locations.

Cruise ships are now being constructed to be extremely accessible. There are many more accessible cabins on board, wider hallways, no barriers to entering cabins, dining rooms with wheelchair table heights, accessible restrooms on all public decks and many more features.

Family members of all ages can find much to do on board, making multigenerational cruise vacations extremely popular. You can make and share memories with everyone. Celebrate family reunions, birthdays, anniversaries, or just being together.

Cruise lines are training their crews to deal with disabilities and there are almost mini-hospitals on board. All cruise ships have medical staff on board to deal with minor health issues that arise. If anything more serious occurs the medical staff will help you get treatment at your destination or help you to med evac home.

Accessible cabins have extra room for maneuvering wheelchairs and storing other equipment you might need. The cabins are constructed so that there are roll in bathrooms and the appointments are wheelchair height for easy access.

There is another plus for those doing physical rehabilitation and exercise regimens. Cruise ships today have well-equipped gyms and spas that you can use to keep up your routine while at sea. The gym is free and there are trainers to assist you if need be. There are fees for the spa services, but the selection of services is extensive.

Cruises are all over the world and major cruise lines change itineraries each year so you can always find someplace different to visit. In most cases you can find accessible excursions in port and the Excursion Desk on the ship will help you identify and book them.

If dietary restrictions and requirements are a concern, cruise lines are especially good at dealing with each person's individual needs. The chefs are trained to work with all food groups and will work with you to prepare individual meals if necessary. It is one of the few places where you can feel confident of tasty and safe meals when traveling.

ALL-INCLUSIVE RESORTS

All-inclusive resorts are also a good vacation choice. They have many of the same features as a cruise. There are activities for all ages, which also makes them wonderful for family and multigenerational vacations.

With all-inclusive resorts you pay one price and everything is included. This includes all food, beverages (alcoholic and non-alcoholic), activities, entertainment, taxes and fees, and gratuities. The only exceptions might be diving and deep sea fishing.

All-inclusive resorts are located in the Caribbean, Mexico, and Central America. They do not exist in the United States or anywhere else in the world right now.

They have accessible rooms and many have lifts to get you into the pool. You can also rent Beach Wheelchairs to get you out onto the sand and into the ocean. As more of these very popular resorts are being constructed and renovated, they are adding more accessible rooms and amenities you can take advantage of. Take a sunset cruise or have a romantic dinner on the beach. Share all kinds of activities with your family.

Some all-inclusive resorts are adult only and some are geared to family vacations. Check with your travel professional to be sure you book the right resort for your needs. In season many airlines have direct flights to the different islands so you need to check the easiest route and what the scheduled dates of non-stop travel are.

DISNEY THEME PARKS AND RESORTS

For young and old alike, Disney resorts are extremely accessible. The parks, hotels and even the rides are easy to navigate. Disney staff are trained to deal with disabilities and to be of assistance throughout the resorts and parks.

Disney now has a tool called the MagicBand that makes special needs travel at Disney even easier. The colorful wristband is an all-in-one device that effortlessly connects you to all the vacation choices you made. The MagicBand enables you to travel lighter. You use it to enter the parks, unlock your Disney Resort hotel room, and buy your food and merchandise. In addition, it gives you FastPass access to all the experiences you've selected. All you do is touch your MagicBand against a sensor called a touch point. This makes it much easier to concentrate on enjoying the fun.

Special needs folks visiting Disney can rent Electric Conveyance Vehicles for a fee of $50.00 daily (Plus $20.00 refundable deposit) at the theme parks and $50.00 (Plus $100.00 refundable deposit) at Downtown Disney. There are a limited number of available vehicles so you should get there early. Specific Disney providers will also rent you equipment that can be delivered to your resort for your use at the resort as well as throughout Disney property.

Disney offers disabled veterans a discount of 30%-40% on Disney resort rooms. Disney Armed Forces Salute also offers discounts on Park Hopper Tickets. You need to be 100% service connected and have the required ID. Your VA Benefits card is not proof of eligibility. You will need a military issued ID card, either a DD Form 1173 or 2765. The ID needs to have the DAVPRM (Disabled Veteran Permanent) code on it.

Service animals are welcome in most locations at Disney, but must have the proper certifications and vaccinations and must remain on a leash or harness at all times. There are animal relief areas usually at (Backstage) locations. You should consult the Guidebook For Guests With Disabilities for details. A good thing is also to check with a host or hostess in each park as you enter.

Of course, you can travel anywhere you desire, but all in all these are the easiest vacations.

The important thing is that you do not sit home and think about it, but get out and enjoy the world we live in.

❧ TRAVELING AS AN AMPUTEE ❧

Travel for an amputee is definitely a challenge, but also VERY POSSIBLE. As with any disability, preparation is the key to a successful vacation.
PLAN - CHECK- and DOUBLE CHECK.

It is always a good idea to have a travel professional trained in special needs travel to help you plan your vacation, and definitely less stressful. Making all the arrangements yourself can be daunting and if you use a travel website on line, there really isn't anyone to guide you or go to if there is a problem. These professionals know **the do's and don'ts and can help you avoid problems that you might not even think of.**

As with any travel, air travel can be a major obstacle, although not insurmountable. The airlines today are making great strides in dealing with special needs, as well as the TSA at the security check in areas. For complete details, check the chapter on Air Travel With A Disability.

Before you travel, check your prosthesis. Make sure your prosthesis is in good condition so you do not have to worry about it while you are away.

If you use a wheelchair and are taking your own wheelchair with you, make sure it is in good working condition also. If you do not wish to take your own, wheelchairs can be rented anywhere in the world and delivered to your location.

It is a good idea to take a doctor's letter with you that describes your disability, as well as your medical history, medications, and your doctor's contact information.

Take two sets of medication with you. If you should lose one or have an unexpected delay, you will be covered.

When going through airport security your prosthesis will most likely set off the alarm. It may be helpful to announce to the TSA agents that you are wearing a prosthesis to avoid surprises. In the majority of cases you should not be asked to remove your prosthesis. If the screener needs to see or touch your prosthesis you can request a private screening. (See our chapter on Air Travel With A Disability).

When booking your flight be sure and ask for a bulkhead seat. These seats are in the front of the plane, have more legroom and are easier to get in and out. If this is not available ask for an aisle seat in the front of the plane with an armrest that swings up out of the way.

Crutches need to be stored under your seat or in the overhead compartment, so collapsible crutches are best for air travel.

Personal wheelchairs and scooters need to be stored in cargo so be sure to take all removable parts, such as cushions, off and take them on board with you. This way they will not get lost. Attached instructions or how to assemble and disassemble the chair or scooter so airlines personnel can help you if need be. An even easier way to deal with this is to wrap the chair or scooter or wheelchair in plastic wrap or bubble wrap so in can be put in cargo intact.

A new popular service that makes travel a luxury is "luggage forwarding". This allows you to save time at the airport by avoiding long check-in lines and skipping the wait at the baggage carousel. Pickup and delivery can be done at your hotel, cruise ship, or vacation home, virtually anywhere in the world. It eliminates carrying heavy, bulky luggage and/ sports equipment. For the extra money it gives you total travel convenience.

A Handbook for Special Needs Travelers

Amtrak provides many services for those with special needs. You can make reservations for accessible bedroom accommodations, transfer seats, wheelchair space, a seat near the restroom and lower-level seating. Although AMTRAK does not offer assigned seating, they will make every attempt to accommodate these requests. Another plus for AMTRAK is that most stations are accessible to passengers with disabilities.

Another option is bus travel. In the United States, Greyhound Bus Lines is your best bet. They have the most accessible buses in the fleet and are willing to assist you at the bus stations. European bus travel is more difficult as there are not as many accessible buses and they might not go everywhere you are planning. (See our chapter on Accessible Bus Travel for further details).

However you choose to travel, I cannot stress enough the importance of planning ahead.Another must is to pack a repair kit. What can be an inconvenience at home can be a disaster in another country.

Hotel chains are now very conscious of special needs. When refurbishing they are adding accessible rooms and bathrooms. Of course, ADA regulations have aided this process.

When you use a hotel, the safest way to book it is to call the hotel directly and explain what you need. The general reservation agents at the 800 number have, most likely, never seen the particular hotel and know very little about its special needs facilities.

If you want to be absolutely certain of what the accessible room and bathroom look like, have the hotel email you a photo. With digital cameras this is very easy to do. If you don't have a computer they can mail it.

When you arrive, if the modern, high fluffy bed is too high, ask the hotel to take the frame off the bed or remove one of the mattresses. These options will lower the bed for easy transfer. If you need a hospital bed, that can be rented and delivered to your hotel.

A cruise is always the most relaxing and easiest vacation for you and/or your family.

You only unpack once and you can enjoy all the ports of call. You can choose excursions that suit your needs and your energy level.

Cruise ships are easy to get around and any equipment you may need can be rented and on board for your use anywhere in the world. If you need an accessible cabin with an accessible bathroom, they are available on all major cruise lines.

Cruise ships are designed to make it easy for you to access many activities, such as pools with lifts and professional stage shows.

Land tours need to be planned more carefully and you may need to be flexible about your expectations so that you are not disappointed with the vacation. But, all in all, most vacations are possible.

In case of emergency make sure you know the locations of hospitals and doctors who speak English, if needed, at your destination. The internet is a good source of information or you can contact the International Association for Medical Assistance to Travelers at 716-754-4883.

Now that we've reviewed some of the major issues facing travel for an amputee, you are armed with much of the knowledge you need to explore the world.

❧ TRAVELING WITH ARTHRITIS ❧

Traveling with arthritis can be difficult at times, but it's important to remember that help is available every step of the way. Just because you have arthritis doesn't mean you can't travel. The key for a successful trip is PREPARATION and understanding your own limitations.

A skilled travel professional familiar with the special requirements of travelers with special needs can considerably improve your travel experience.

It's important to begin planning as early as possible so your travel professional can help you deal with any obstacles. They are trained to make the process easier.

AIR TRAVEL
Air travel is often the preferred way to go. Dealing with the airlines can be stressful, but it is manageable. If you think you will need help at the airport's security checkpoint, you can call the special TSA toll-free hotline for those with disabilities at 855-787-2227. Make sure to call at least 72 hours ahead of travel so they can coordinate support with a customer service manager. (See our article on Air Travel With A Disability)

TRAIN TRAVEL
For people with arthritis, traveling by train may be easier than by plane. You can reserve accessible seats, wheelchair space, or overnight accommodations in an accessible room. If you have medicine that needs to be kept cool, Amtrak can provide ice for your container. There are dining cars and accessible bathrooms. (See our article on Accessible Train Travel)

BUS TRAVEL
Buses can present a challenge. Many do not have lifts, so be sure to check ahead of time. Bus line itineraries vary so find one that makes frequent enough stops for your comfort. You may also be required to have a doctor's letter to get a discount for a traveling companion. Check all rules and regulations before you buy your tickets. (See our article on Accessible Bus Travel)

CRUISE TRAVEL
Cruise lines have been in the vanguard of providing special services and accommodations for special needs travelers. That's why they can be a great option for your trip. When you travel on board a crusie ship

- You unpack only once and you get to visit a variety of ports
- Your cruise ship will provide assistance boarding and disembarking the ship
- Your travel professional can rent whatever equipment you might need.
- The equipment is placed on board for your use throughout the cruise – and this can be done anywhere in the world.

All major cruise lines have ships with accessible cabins and accessible bathrooms. Getting around the ship is easy and dining tables are wheelchair height. There are all levels of excursions in port so you can choose ones that meet your interests and abilities.

STAYING AT A HOTEL

When looking for a hotel room, location is very important. Call the hotel directly and ask for a room near the elevator. Don't use the general reservation number because that is in a central location and the agents may not be familiar with the individual hotels. If you have trouble climbing steps, a bed and breakfast may not be a good selection, because they generally do not have elevators. Your best bet is a major hotel chain.

PACKING FOR YOU TRIP

Pack as light as you can for any trip and make sure to bring only what you can handle. Think about what you will be doing, the climate at your destination and pack accordingly. Make sure you pack all your prescriptions and/or over-the-counter medications that you need in your carryon luggage. Be sure they are all clearly labeled. Never put prescription drugs or medications in your checked baggage.

If you need more than you can easily handle, you might want to look into shipping ahead. A new popular service that makes travel a luxury is "luggage forwarding". This allows you to save time at the airport by avoiding long check-in lines and skipping the wait at the baggage carousel. Pickup and delivery can be done at your hotel, cruise ship, or vacation home, virtually anywhere in the world. It eliminates carrying heavy, bulky luggage and/or sports equipment. For the extra money it gives you total travel convenience.

Take a brief medical history, a list of medications, and contact information for your primary care doctor and rheumatologist. It is also wise to take your health insurance information. (See our article on Why Do I Need Travel Insurance)

In case of an emergency make sure you know the locations of hospitals and doctors who speak English, if needed, at your destination. The internet is a good source of information or you can contact the International Association for Medical Assistance to Travelers at 716-754-4883.

When planning your vacations consider the environment and climate of your destination. If you hurt more on cold and wet days, you may not want to travel to places with a winter climate. Conversely, if you do not do well in heat and humidity, tropical destinations like the Caribbean during the summer may not be a good idea.

You might also want to plan to arrive a day early to rest up and restore your energy before beginning your activities.

Remember, travel doesn't have to be a pain.
Proper planning and preparation can make the difference between
a frustrating trip and a successful one.
Think ahead.

⋘ TRAVELING WITH DIABETES ⋙

Whenever you're on vacation, wherever you decide to go, preparation is the key to having more fun and less stress. Here's what you'll need to do before you travel:

FIRST, visit or call your health care provider to make sure you have sufficient medications for the length of your trip and to develop a schedule to keep your injections current. This is particularly important if you are going into a different time zone.

Then create a list of diabetes-related supplies and calculate how much of each you will need. THEN DOUBLE IT!

Take emergency prescriptions with you and a doctor's note explaining why you need all of your various medications and supplies. This is no longer required by TSA, but it may help make your trip through airport security easier.

If you need immunization shots, get those three to four weeks before you travel, as shots may upset your blood sugar levels.

It is always a good idea to travel with your supplies in a clear plastic bag so the TSA agents can easily see them. Display them in an obvious place in the TSA bins on the security conveyor belt and point them out to the security team with an explanation of the objects. If you do this you are not likely to have a problem. If you are traveling with a companion it is also a good idea to give some of your diabetes supplies to that person in the rare case that something happens to your carryon bag. This will ensure that you have the medications you need until you can get a new supply.

If you are nervous about going through the metal detector with your insulin pump, notify the Security Officer that you are wearing an insulin pump and would like a full-body pat-down instead. Make sure the agent understands that the insulin pump cannot be removed.

If you are traveling by air, special meals can be ordered ahead. So be certain to call in advance of your flight to order a diabetic, low fat, or low cholesterol meal. If by any chance the airline doesn't offer such a meal, you can bring your own food with you on board.

Depending on the length of the flight you might want to bring your own food on board anyway, just in case there is a glitch and the airline does not have your pre-ordered special meal.

When drawing up your doses of insulin on the plane, don't inject air into the bottle. Most likely the air on your plane will be pressurized.

Reduce your risk of blood clots by moving around every hour or so.

Whatever you decide to do on your vacation, plan it so that you have time to rest during the day. Don't over tax yourself.

CRUISE VACATIONS are perhaps the most relaxing type of vacation. Cruise ships provide as much or as little activity as you choose. Meals are much easier to manage and snacks are always readily available. If you are traveling aboard a ship, it is good to know that cruise ships are especially good at providing you with personalized meals that are both healthy and tasty.

RESORTS can also provide you with a high level and comfort and relaxation. You can use your resort as a base and take day trips or excursions without packing and unpacking as you move from one location to another.

No matter where you are, or what type of vacation you're planning, do not be afraid to ask for help. People want to be of assistance, but they can't assist you if you don't alert them to your needs. Getting the help you need could make the difference between a great vacation and a not-so-great vacation.

A popular service that makes travel a luxury is "luggage forwarding". This allows you to save time at the airport by avoiding long check-in lines and skipping the wait at the baggage carousel. Pickup and delivery can be done at your hotel, cruise ship, or vacation home, virtually anywhere in the world. It eliminates carrying heavy, bulky luggage and/or sports equipment. For the extra money it gives you total travel convenience.

If you are considering traveling with a tour operator, be sure the tour allows for time on your own. If you are sightseeing on your own it's easier to plan down time. Cruise ships and resorts can help you choose appropriate excursions.

In case of emergency make sure you know the locations of hospitals and doctors who speak English, if needed, at your destination. The internet is a good source of information or you can contact the International Association for Medical Assistance to Travelers at 716-754-4883.

Pack the right footwear. If you get new shoes for the trip break them in beforehand and make sure there aren't any problems with the way they fit. Buy walking or hiking shoes at a store that has experience fitting people with diabetes, especially if you have lost feeling in your toes or feet. Remember to be careful of hot pavement by pools and hot sand on the beach. And never go barefoot.

Long layovers, missed connections or delays on the runway can make it difficult to get the food you need promptly, causing stress and a serious low. Make sure you are well prepared by packing snacks like whole grain and/or peanut butter crackers and granola or trail mix bars in your carryon bag.

Different countries have different styles of preparing, seasoning and cooking foods, so check out the cuisine before you travel. Preview the most popular foods, find out how they are prepared and what ingredients are used. This will give you a better idea of how to control your carbs. And it's worth repeating, wherever you go, always keep a healthy snack on hand just in case you encounter food you're unsure of or experience low blood sugar.

Remember, it's your vacation. Have a great time. And relax—you deserve it!

✿ VACATIONING ON DIALYSIS ✿

Just because you're on dialysis doesn't mean you have to give up the excitement of travel. You can still enjoy all those memorable times with family and friends.

You can go on a cruise, vacation abroad, take a road trip or visit famous attractions and entertainment spots. And wherever you go you can still take care of all your dialysis needs.

Travelers have several dialysis options:
- Visit a dialysis center at your destination
- Bring your own dialysis equipment with you
- Rent your equipment and arrange for delivery to your destination(s).

But however you choose to travel, and wherever you choose to go, the key to a successful trip is planning. It may take some time, and you may have to be a little more flexible, but once your plans are completed you're practically on your way to an enjoyable, exciting vacation.

SOME SUGGESTED VACATION DESTINATIONS

Las Vegas is the most dialysis-friendly city in the US. It is very easy to find conveniently located dialysis centers in the greater Las Vegas area. Las Vegas also offers more accessible hotel rooms than any other city.

Cruises, on the other hand, are by far the easiest for anyone on dialysis. That's because cruise lines have organized special cruises that are set up for dialysis patients.

Cruise lines are also used to meeting special dietary requirements. You should definitely bring a list of foods you can and cannot eat so you stay on your kidney diet. And don't be afraid to ask servers about additional food options, like vegetarian plates or protein-enriched foods.

Those on peritoneal dialysis (PD) can bring their supplies on the cruise. And you should always bring extra supplies in case of any additional travel days.

A cruise can enable you to make memories with family and friends that you would never have thought possible.

Walt Disney World in Orlando, Florida is a wonderful place to bring the family. There is so much to see and do so you will never be bored. And you have two coasts to choose from: Disney Resort in Anaheim, CA and Disney World in Orlando, FL. Each destination is ready, willing and able to help meet your special dialysis needs.

Busch Gardens theme parks in Florida and Virginia are another popular dialysis-friendly destination.

And there are many museums, botanical gardens, zoos, and amazing landmarks for you to include in your vacation plans.

Road trips and camping may need a little more planning, but are a lot of fun and can be done conveniently.

No matter what style of vacation you choose and wherever your destination, careful planning is the key to a successful trip. You should contact your travel professional as soon as you decide that travel plans are in your future. The longer the lead time the easier and less stressful it will be.

Your travel professional can help you design an itinerary that takes into account the locations of dialysis centers. It is simply a matter of deciding when and where you need to have your dialysis treatments and planning around that.

Dialysis center reservations should be made at least three months in advance to ensure that you get a space. If you are on home dialysis, remember to make room for your PD or HHD machine and supplies in your luggage. If the trip is more than 10 days, we might arrange for supplies to be delivered to your destination so you do not have to carry it with you.

Once these details are taken care of you can continue to plan all the fun parts of your trip and enjoy the anticipation of a wonderful time.

If you are flying to your destination you can make the security check-in at the airport much easier. Just put all of your medical supplies in one bag and label them MEDICAL SUPPLIES in an obvious place. You will not be charged for that medical bag. But if you put even one piece of clothing in it, then it is not considered medical and you will be charged. Separating and labeling your supplies can also speed up the security process because the TSA agent does not have to dig through your luggage to find everything.

SPECIAL PLANNING FOR TRAVELING ABROAD

First of all, Medicare and most insurance companies do not cover dialysis treatment costs incurred while traveling abroad. You should price these treatments beforehand so you have an idea of the costs and can plan your trip accordingly. Your travel professional can help by providing you with information on the proper insurance for your needs.

Dialysis centers are located around the world so if you have the money it can all be coordinated. Peritoneal dialysis patients can have their supplies delivered to their hotel, or whatever their destination. Planning with lots of lead time is critical. And you should definitely plan to bring some extra supplies to cover you in case there any travel glitches. For home hemodialysis patients, you can take the NxStage machine abroad, but there is no support for it if you have a problem. You will be on your own for supplies or a substitute machine. But once again, with time and advanced planning, this can be dealt with.

Thanks to advancements in the travel industry, you are now free to enjoy cruising, land trips and much more. Now you can take your own photos instead of waiting to see the ones family and friends bring back.

You have no excuse for staying home.
Memories with loved ones remain with you always,
so get out there and make some.

TRAVELING WITH
☾ A HEARING IMPAIRMENT ☽

If you are one of the at least 20 million people in the United States with hearing loss it does not mean you can't enjoy a great travel vacation. It just means you will have to plan your trip a little more carefully.

Working with a travel professional who is an expert at special needs travel will help you avoid all the pitfalls. A trained travel professional can guide you through the planning process and help eliminate much of the strain. Little things can make a big difference, such as e-mailing you all the confirmations so you can make a packet of the information you will need to take with you

MAKING A LIST—CHECKING IT TWICE

The first step in planning a trip is to make a complete list of everything you need to pack. You make a list for the supermarket, so why not make one for your trip? Medications? Check. Hearing aid batteries? Check. Power converters for overseas travel? Check. Writing it all down keeps you from forgetting all the important items you'll need for your trip.

ALERT THE STAFF

Let folks know your needs all along the way so staff can help you and alert you to any changes that might impact your trip. Make use of all available apps that will give you alerts and texts on your cell phone. Airlines, Amtrak, hotels, cruise lines, tour companies are all getting on the bandwagon with apps.

GET IT IN WRITING

When dealing with the airlines be sure that the assistance you require is confirmed in writing on your ticket or itinerary. Staff may have Deaf Awareness Training or sign language. Consider reserving aisle seats for easier communication with the flight staff if you choose to fly. Health, safety and general information can be provided in writing. Your hearing dog is allowed to travel with you free of charge, but remember your dog will need proper documentation and vaccinations

PACK YOUR MEDS

Pack any medications and hearing aid batteries and supplies in your carryon bag so they are readily available. If you have Menieres disease or your ears feel "funny" on take-off and landing, there are special ear plugs that can help maintain balanced ear pressure, helping avoid triggering Vertigo and Tinnitus.

In most cases, hearing aids worn on or in the ears will not set off alarms at airports during security screening. Body-worn hearing aids and personal listening devices may however, so they should be packed in your carryon bag. Security screeners will not harm any of these devices. (See the chapter on Air Travel With A Disability).

When checking into a hotel, carry printed copies of all reservations with dates and prices. Inform the front desk receptionist that you are hearing impaired. THIS IS VERY IMPORTANT IN CASE OF EMERGENCY. Some major hotel chains may provide visual alerting devices to help you recognize the ring of the phone, a knock on the door or fire/emergency alarm. Be sure to make arrangements for these and any other needs in advance.

MANY ORGANIZATIONS WOULD LOVE TO HELP YOU

Contact your local organization for the hearing impaired for the address of a possible counterpart agency at your destination. They may have a TTY and interpretation service if needed.

Keep paper and pens handy for communication.

The Society For Accessible Travel & Hospitality (SATH) suggests that "The International Travelers Point and Conversion Guide" is a useful tool, especially abroad. The 4" by 5" booklet has pictures related to 6 main topics: services, shopping, sports & entertainment, transportation, accommodations, and food items. To order a copy, send $6.95 including shipping to ArnMoor Publishing, 3956 Town Center Blvd., Suite 104, Orlando, FL 32837; Tel: (407)855-5944 or Fax (407) 855-5958.

DO YOU TRAVEL WITH A SERVICE ANIMAL?

If you travel with a service animal you will need to carry documentation certifying your animal's special status, as well as all veterinary health certifications that are required by the countries you plan to visit. Some island states have strict anti-rabies laws which restrict the entrance of all animals including service animals. Some countries have severe regulations and prolonged quarantines. These include the State of Hawaii, Australia, New Zealand, Ireland and the United Kingdom. Be sure to check the regulations for each country you plan to visit. This information can be obtained from consulates, or sometimes from the airline you are using. A trained travel professional can help guide you through the necessary forms.

The leather-covered harness, leash, and collar of guide dogs may be made of stainless steel and will activate the metal detector when the dog goes through the airport security check. If this happens, an airport employee will hold the dog while you go through the metal detector, or you and the dog can be checked by a hand-operated detector.

ARE YOU CONSIDERING A CRUISE?

Cruise lines are especially good at dealing with special needs travelers. Before boarding, complete a Guest Special Needs Form so the staff can customize your accommodations to meet you specific needs. A portable room kit is available for your stateroom upon request. It include a visual-tactile alert system that provides alerts for door knocking, telephone ringing, alarm clock and smoke detector. A TTY (teletypewriter) is available for your stateroom upon request and it is linked with the TTY at the Guest Relations Desk to assist with all your stateroom needs.

Amplified telephones are available in staterooms and public areas and Assistive Listening systems are located in most theaters on board.

Closed-captioned televisions are available in staterooms on most ships. While only select programs may be captioned, all safety videos are.

DO YOU USE SIGN LANGUAGE TO COMMUNICATE?

Sign language interpreting services can be requested for deaf guests who use American Sign Language (ASL) as their primary means of communication. Sign language interpreting is provided at specific events and times, so check with your particular cruise line. The request for sign language interpreting must be made at least 60 days before departure so be sure to make arrangements very early in your planning process.

GET IT IN WRITING

All special requests should be confirmed with your intended cruise line BEFORE you make your deposit. This will eliminate a lot of disappointment and distress. And if possible, make sure you get your confirmations in writing.

TRAVEL INSURANCE

Another consideration in your planning process is travel insurance. If you need to make a last-minute cancellation it is the only way to get your money back. In addition, you should always insure for pre-existing health conditions when you travel—particularly abroad. Medicare does not cover you outside the United States, U.S. Virgin Islands or Puerto Rico. (See the chapter on Why Do I Need Travel Insurance?)

A little planning and forethought can make a big difference in the success of your trip. You can enjoy all the wonders of travel.

So, get out there and start making memories!

TRAVELING WITH
◌⧔ MULTIPLE SCLEROSIS ⧓◌

Traveling with MS has many of the same issues as traveling with any other special need. But there are important differences.

In reality you can go anywhere. Photograph the animals in Africa, see the volcanoes in Hawaii or shop in Hong Kong. It's a big world out there and there is no reason why you can't get out and see it all.

THE SECRET IS IN THE PLANNING.

Start planning as early as you can.

Consulting a travel expert familiar with your condition can make a big difference. Travel professionals have the expertise necessary to help you avoid the pitfalls that can ruin your special time. Booking your vacation on the web is very risky and if you have a problem there is no one to talk to.

Make sure you
- Know your limitations and pace yourself accordingly
- Don't over schedule yourself
- Allow enough time to rest
- Don't get overheated or dehydrated

If you are planning to travel with a tour company be sure the itinerary gives you enough free time to rest if you need to.

Since MS may not be immediately apparent, it is best to be up front and honest all along the way when you travel. This is especially true when dealing with the airlines. Most people want to be of assistance but they must be made aware of your special needs.

You should call the special TSA toll-free hotline for those with disabilities at 855-787-2227 at least 72 hours ahead of travel so it they can coordinate support with a customer service manager at the airport's security checkpoint. (See our chapter on Air Travel with a Disability for more details)

Traveling by train may be easier than by plane. You can reserve accessible seats, wheelchair space, or overnight accommodations in an accessible room. If you have medicine that needs to be kept cool, Amtrak can provide ice for your container. There are also dining cars and accessible bathrooms. (See our chapter on Accessible Train Travel for more details).

Another option is traveling by bus. In the United States, Greyhound Bus Lines is your best bet. They have the most accessible buses in the fleet and are willing to assist you at the bus stations. European bus travel is more difficult as there are not as many accessible buses and they might not go everywhere you are planning. (See our chapter on Accessible Bus Travel for further details)

No matter how you travel, pack as lightly as you can and don't take anything you can't handle yourself. Think very carefully about what you really need. Think about your planned activities and your destination and pack accordingly.

A new popular service that makes travel a luxury is "luggage forwarding". This allows you to save time at the airport by avoiding long check-in lines and skipping the wait at the baggage carousel. Pickup and delivery can be done at your hotel, cruise ship, or vacation home, virtually anywhere in the world. It eliminates carrying heavy, bulky luggage and/or sports equipment. For the extra money it gives you total travel convenience.

Make sure you pack all your prescriptions and/or over-the-counter medications in your carryon luggage. Be sure they are all clearly labeled. Never put them in your checked baggage. If you require excess baggage assistance, consider having those items shipped to your destination.

A cruise is always the most relaxing and easiest vacation for you and/or your family.
- You unpack only once and you can enjoy all the ports of call
- You can choose excursions that suit your needs and your energy level.
- Cruise ships are easy to get around and any equipment you may need can be rented and on board for your use anywhere in the world.
- If you need an accessible cabin with an accessible bathroom, they are available on all major cruise lines.
- Cruise ships are designed to make it easy for you access many activities, such as pools with lifts and professional stage shows.

All-inclusive resorts in the Caribbean and Mexico are also a good choice.
- Again, you unpack only once
- All of the food and beverages, activities and entertainment are included
- You can be as busy or as laid back as you choose
- Resorts have activities and entertainment for all ages, so don't hesitate to travel with the family. Or If you prefer you can book an adult-only resort.

All-inclusive resorts are very busy in season and at holidays. If you want a less crowded scene try traveling on the shoulder or off-season. Check with your travel professional to select the dates that are best for you.

Whenever you travel be sure to have the proper travel insurance. It allows you to go travel with peace of mind. And you won't have to worry about medical or financial travel issues. (See the article on Why Do I Need Travel Insurance? for full details.) Be sure to take a copy of your policy with you when you travel.

In case of emergency make sure you know the locations of hospitals and doctors who speak English, if needed, at your destination. The internet is a good source of information or you can contact the International Association for Medical Assistance to Travelers at 716-754-4883.

Several times in this article I mentioned consulting a travel professional. The professional should be skilled in special needs travel to make your planning process truly easy and your travel safe. After you tell them what you want and answer some questions, they do all the leg work. They are experts at planning and preparation. And they are also up to date on the many issues and laws that may impact your trip.

As we said earlier, it's a big world out there, so get out and enjoy it!

TRAVELING WITH
⊂⊗ PARKINSON'S DISEASE ⟋◯

Most people with Parkinson's Disease can travel with proper planning. The key to the planning is to begin as early as possible. This way no detail is missed or forgotten.

It is also a good idea to use a travel professional who is trained to work with special needs so that the whole process is less stressful.

Be sure that you have the proper travel insurance with pre-existing medical condition coverage and med evac if you need to be airlifted home. For further details about travel insurance see our chapter on Why Do I Need Travel Insurance?

Take a copy of your medical history with you and ask your neurologist for the name of a doctor where you are traveling in case of a problem.

The National Parkinson Foundation will send you FREE OF CHARGE, an Aware in Care Kit. This kit contains many items you should pack in your carryon bag. These include a Medication Form to list your medical conditions and medications, a medical alert bracelet and a list of important things to remember when caring for a person with Parkinson's Disease.

In planning your trip be sure to allow time to rest during the day. And very importantly rest the day before you leave and the day after you arrive.

TRAVEL METHODS

Whether you are going by air, train, or bus you need to treat your medications carefully. Carry all medication in its original bottle, with the name of the drug and your doctor on the label. Two sets of meds are always good in case some is lost or stolen. Bring copies of all of your prescriptions, why and how you take them, and your doctor's contact information.

Always carry your medication with you in your carry bag, including snacks, water or juices to take them with. If you are changing time zones you should continue to take your medications as prescribed, with the same timing. If it is easier for you, you might consider wearing two watches with your current time and your home time.

Air travel is usually the most stressful part of the trip. You should definitely check in early to take care of all the flight details and have time to wait comfortably to board the plane. It is a good idea to request wheelchair assistance to go from the curbside to the plane and back to the curbside when you arrive. It can be quite a distance and you do not want to get tired before you even start your trip. When making your reservation you should request an aisle seat close to the bathroom. For more details about air travel, see the chapter on Air Travel with a Disability.

If you choose to travel by train, Amtrak is the most accommodating for folks with special needs in the United States. Amtrak is proud of the strides they have made for accessibility. The train stations are accessible and many features on the train are also. There are accessible bathrooms and special seats for transfer from a wheelchair.

Rail Europe will most probably be your choice in Europe.

They have accessible seating and accessible bedrooms if you need to travel overnight. Most train stations have easy access and you can get easily to the train for boarding. Of course, you must plan ahead and double check all your reservations and requests for assistance. For further details see our chapter on Accessible Train Travel.

Another option is bus travel. In the United States, Greyhound Bus Lines is your best bet. They have the most accessible buses in the fleet and are willing to assist you at the bus stations. European bus travel is more difficult as there are not as many accessible buses and they might not go everywhere you are planning. (see our chapter on Accessible Bus Travel for further details.)

CRUISE VACATIONS

Cruise vacations make it easy for you to do as much or as little as you want. They are relaxing and you only have to unpack once. You can explore the various ports of call or just stay on board. If you decide to explore there are now various levels of excursions offered, including accessible ones, so you just have to choose. If you just want to wander around on your own you can do that too.

Cruise ships now have more handicapped accessible cabins, although they are still limited. If you have mobility issues you need to book as early as possible to be sure to secure one. The cabins have extra room for wheelchairs and roll in bathrooms. The interior of the cabin itself is wheelchair height with no barriers.

The ships themselves have wider corridors, more accessible bathrooms, wheelchair height dining, lifts in the pools and much more to add to your enjoyment. The cruise experience is great for you and the whole family. There are activities for every age group no matter what they like to do.

There is another plus for those doing physical rehabilitation or exercise regimens. Cruise ships today have well-equipped gyms and spas that you can use to keep up your routine while at sea. The gym is free and there are trainers to assist you if need be. There are fees for the spa services, but the selection of services is extensive.

When planning a hotel stay, you need to be more diligent. Even with ADA regulations, things are not the same at each hotel. You need to ask them what exactly accessible means. If you aren't sure after asking, ask for a photo of the room and bathroom. Digital photography makes this very easy to do and you will not be disappointed when you get there. Never call the 800 reservation number to book your room. These folks have most likely never seen your hotel choice. Always call the hotel directly for the best answers to your questions and concerns.

If you need medical equipment such as a lift, hospital bed, wheelchair or scooter, these and much more can be rented and delivered anywhere in the world. You will find them in your cruise cabin or hotel room. You use them on vacation and simply leave them to be picked up by the rental company. It is as easy as that.

A new popular service that makes travel a luxury is "luggage forwarding". This allows you to save time at the airport by avoiding long check-in lines and skipping the wait at the baggage carousel. Pickup and delivery can be done at your hotel, cruise ship, or vacation home, virtually anywhere in the world. IT eliminates carrying heavy, bulky luggage and/or sports equipment. For the extra money it gives you total travel convenience.

If you have physical challenges you might want to consider bringing a professional aide along to help you. If traveling with the family and depending on your budget, family members can all contribute to the cost, not burdening any one member. Bringing an aide along allows everyone to enjoy their vacation and have all needs properly taken care of.

In case of emergency make sure you know the locations of hospitals and doctors who speak English, if needed, at your destination. The internet is a good source of information or you can contact the International Association for Medical Assistance to Travelers at 716-754-4883.

Now that we have reviewed some of the major challenges to traveling, you can see that it is easier than you thought. You must plan and take care, but you do not have to stay at home. If all this seems too daunting, seek the help of a travel professional who is trained to assist with special needs travel.

So, get packing and get going!

TRAVELING WITH
POST STROKE AND APHASIA

Just because you have experienced a stroke, with or without aphasia, does not mean you need to remain homebound. The same new equipment and options that help travelers with other disabilities are now available to you.

With proper planning you can share all the fun and excitement of travel with your family and friends.

Of course, before you travel, you should check with your doctor. Once you have the green light, then you can start planning.

The first thing you should do is make a list of your medical issues and all the things you would like to do on your vacation. Then you should share them with a travel professional trained to work with your special needs. This is important because he/she can help you plan a safe and easy vacation and help eliminate much of the stress.

A very important part of the planning process is getting the appropriate travel insurance. It's important to have a policy with pre-existing conditions included, so that should you need medical assistance, you are covered. For complete details about travel insurance see the chapter Why Do I Need Travel Insurance.

Through my years working with special needs travelers, I have found that those with aphasia especially enjoy traveling in a group. It is comforting to have the aid of others and a way to share the fun. Traveling alone with aphasia can be tricky if the aphasia is severe, so in that case it might be best to travel with a companion. If you are going alone you might create a name tag. On the front you can put "My Name Is ------" and on the back say "I Have Aphasia" and then a brief description of what it is so others understand how to help you. It would also be good to make up a card with all the details of your trip, such as what airport and flight, the name of the hotel, etc. That way the taxi driver, airline and hotel personnel can easily assist you. (See our chapter on Air Travel With a Disability for more details). **In all cases you should take a medical card with you also that has all your medications listed.**

Airlines have medical restrictions that you will need to comply with. The Aerospace Medical Association suggests that you should not fly for at least two weeks after a stroke— but it's your physician who should make the final call.

When booking a flight, be sure to request
- an extra legroom aisle seat so you can move your legs and feet
- a non-stop flight

If you have to make a connection get extra time between flights so you do not have to rush to another gate or connecting terminal.

PACKING FOR YOUR TRIP

Try to pack lightly and take only one bag to check and one carryon bag. Make sure the checked bag has wheels so you do not have to carry it around the airport. Always carry your medication with you in your carry bag, including snacks, water or juices to take them with.

TRAVELING BY TRAIN

If you choose to travel by train, Amtrak is the most accommodating for travelers with special needs in the United States. Rail Europe is your best choice for European travel. They have accessible seating and accessible bedrooms if you need to travel overnight. Most train stations have easy access and you can get easily to the train for boarding. Of course, you must plan ahead and double check all your reservations and requests for assistance. For further details see our chapter on Accessible Train Travel.

TRAVELING BY BUS

Another option is bus travel. In the United States, Greyhound Bus Lines is your best bet. They have the most accessible buses in the fleet and are willing to assist you at the bus stations. European bus travel is more difficult as there are not as many accessible buses and they might not go everywhere you are planning. (See our chapter on Accessible Bus Travel for further details.

HAVING YOUR LUGGAGE MEET YOU WHEN YOU ARRIVE

A new popular service that makes travel easier is "luggage forwarding". This service allows you to save time at the airport by avoiding long check-in lines and skipping the wait at the baggage carousel. Pickup and delivery can be done at your hotel, cruise ship, or vacation home, virtually anywhere in the world. It eliminates carrying heavy, bulky luggage and/or sports equipment. For the extra money it gives you total travel convenience

CRUISE TRAVEL

If the aphasia is less than severe, with the proper planning and written instructions and details, you can certainly hit the trail. The easiest vacation, for sure, is a cruise. Everything is at your fingertips on a cruise and you won't have to change hotel rooms. You can be as busy as you want to be or you can just relax and enjoy the journey. If you need medical equipment such as a wheelchair, scooter, lift, etc., this can be rented and delivered to the ship for your use on your vacation. When you are ready to disembark, just leave it in your cabin. The rental company will be responsible for retrieving it.

There is another plus for those doing rehabilitation and exercise regimens. Cruise ships today have well-equipped gyms and spas that you can use to keep up your routine while at sea. The gym is free and there are trainers to assist you if need be. There are fees for the spa services, but the selection of services is extensive.

TRAVELING BY LAND

If you are on a land trip, rental equipment can be delivered to your hotel room anywhere in the world. This certainly makes traveling easier and more convenient.

If there is a loss of mobility from the stroke then the rules for walker, wheelchair and scooter travel come into play. In that case the advice provided in this handbook covers air, train and bus travel.

MIND YOUR MEDICATIONS

However you travel, you need to treat your medications carefully. Carry all medication in its original bottle, with the name of the drug and your doctor on the label. Two sets of meds are always good in case some is lost or stolen. Bring a list of all of your prescriptions, why and how your take them, and your doctor's contact information.

In case of emergency make sure you know the locations of hospitals and doctors who speak English, if needed, at your destination. The internet is a good source of information or you can contact the International Association for Medical Assistance to Travelers at 716 754-4883.

TAKE IT EASY

However you choose to travel, whatever activities you plan at your destination, be sure to plan for time to rest between activities. You do not want to put extra stress on your body so that you do not enjoy your trip to the fullest.

The last thing you need to pack is your sense of humor!!
It's an indispensable item for every traveler.

TRAVELING WITH
⟨ SPINAL CORD INJURY ⟩

If you've been dreaming about a special trip, family vacations, anniversary celebration, or just a quick getaway, don't let your spinal cord injury stop you from the experience, the enjoyment and the fun.

The travel and hospitality industries have stepped up to help those with physical disabilities enjoy vacations with family and friends. You can take a cruise, join an African safari or tour Europe. THEY ARE ALL ACCESSIBLE.

TAKING A CRUISE
The easiest vacation for those with spinal cord injury is, by far, a cruise.
- Cruise ships are now being constructed to accommodate wheelchairs.
- There are many more accessible cabins than ever before.
- Cabins are designed with roll-in bathrooms and showers with adequate room for maneuvering a wheelchair.
- Storage space can be easily accessed from your wheelchair.
- Public areas of cruise ships are also very accessible.
- Corridors are wider and dining tables are perfect wheelchair height.
- Cruise lines will even provide pier assistance to help you embark and disembark from the ship.

If you need a wheelchair or transport chair it may be easier and more convenient to rent. The chair will be delivered to your cabin for your use during the cruise, on and off the ship. And when your cruise is completed it will be removed from your cabin.

You can also rent other equipment you may need, such as oxygen, a hospital bed, a lift—pretty much whatever you need to make your journey safe and comfortable.

And, believe it or not, these items are available all over the world, and at very reasonable cost, regardless of which cruise you select.

As each ship and itinerary is different, you should seek the assistance of a travel professional to help you choose the ship and cruise that best meet your needs.

Once you've made your selection, your travel professional can help you secure any special equipment you may need to make your vacation easy and effortless.

River cruises are not the same. At this time the ships are not accessible. But that may change very soon. A major effort is being made to change this in a year or two, so it is something you can look forward to.
- River cruise lines are looking into improved docking facilities so that embarking and disembarking are easy and safe.
- The river cruise lines are also exploring ways to make excursions accessible.

TRAVELING BY AIR
Air travel is of great concern to most folks with special needs. So you'll be glad to know that airlines are working hard to make it easier for you. Changes in TSA rules have

eliminated some of the challenges and have eased the check-in process. But you still need to be aware of some issues you may encounter.

For example, if you have a long flight and use a catheter, you may want to take a connecting flight so you can get off the plane to take care of your personal needs.

For more detailed information be sure to read our article on Air Travel With a Disability.

TRAVELING BY TRAIN

Traveling by train may be easier than by plane. You can reserve accessible seats, wheelchair space, or overnight accommodations in an accessible room. If you have medicine that needs to be kept cool, Amtrak can provide ice for your container. There are also dining cars and accessible bathrooms. (See our chapter on Accessible Train Travel for more details)

TRAVELING BY BUS

Another option is traveling by bus. In the United States, Greyhound Bus Lines is your best bet. They have the most accessible buses in the fleet and are willing to assist you at the bus stations. European bus travel is more difficult as there are not as many accessible buses and they might not go everywhere you are planning. (See our chapter on Accessible Bus Travel for further details.)

VACATIONING AT A RESORT

The new all-inclusive resorts in the Caribbean and Mexico are great choices, whether you just want to get away from it all and relax, or you want a family vacation for all ages. These resorts have activities for everyone. Or you can skip the activities and relax at the pool or on the beach. The beach? Yes, there are now "beach wheelchairs" that allow you to go on the sand and get right into the ocean.

Disney Resorts are the champions at dealing with special needs. All Disney hotels and parks are ADA compliant.

As with anything else, no two resorts are the same. So you should seek the advice of a travel professional familiar with the facilities at each resort, to help you determine the resort that is best for your special vacation.

No matter how you choose to travel, a new popular service that makes travel a luxury is "luggage forwarding". This allows you to save time at the airport by avoiding long check-in lines and skipping the wait at the baggage carousel. Pickup and delivery can be done at your hotel, cruise ship, or vacation home, virtually anywhere in the world. It eliminates carrying heavy, bulky luggage and/or sports equipment. For the extra money it gives you total travel convenience.

You can make as many memories as you want and share experiences with your family and friends. You don't have to sit home and wait for the vacation pictures to arrive. You can make your own pictures—and memories. So go ahead and plan that anniversary trip or family reunion, that special vacation or weekend get-away. You need it. You deserve it. And the travel industry is doing everything it can to help you do it.

The most important thing to remember is that you CAN travel!

TRAVELING WITH
⟨⟨ A VISUAL IMPAIRMENT ⟩⟩

Traveling with a visual impairment can be a challenge, but proper preparation will make a world of difference in the success your trip. The most important first step, after you've selected your destination, is to learn all you can about the location you've chosen.

Of course, you can make all the calls and reservations for yourself, but the easiest and least stressful approach is to take advantage of the services of a trained travel professional–one who understands the requirements of special needs travelers. A trained travel professional can definitely help you avoid pitfalls and make your vacation more fun.

It can be very helpful to get your itinerary and directions written down before you leave–and be sure to carry them with you. That way if you need any help you can just show them to someone else. Be sure to include the name and address of your hotel, cruise ship, etc. Each and every detail of your itinerary should be on your list so there are no mistakes and no confusion. Once you have all your trip documentation completed, put three packets together: one for your carryon bag, one for your luggage and one to leave with a family member or friend as a backup. The packets should also include copies of your passport and travel insurance policy.

Don't be shy about asking for help at any time during your trip. I have always found that people want to be helpful, but they can't help if YOU don't ask. If you have a cane, carry it with you, whether you plan to use it or not. Your cane helps alert others that you are visually impaired.

THE IMPORTANCE OF TRAVEL INSURANCE

No one should travel without travel insurance. It can protect against losing money if you need to cancel at the last minute. Without it you could lose the total amount you paid. The travel industry relies very heavily on travel insurance programs. Your travel professional can help you find the policy that's right for you. But any policy you select needs to cover pre-existing conditions and medical evacuation in case you need to be rushed back to the United States. Remember, Medicare does not cover you outside the United States, U.S. Virgin Islands and Puerto Rico. (See the chapter on Why Do I Need Travel Insurance?).

TRAVEL BY AIR

If at all possible make due with only carryon luggage: you can't lose the luggage you carry with you.If you can't get by with carryon luggage, you might consider shipping your luggage to your destination and back. There are many companies that will pick up and deliver your luggage anywhere in the world. Your travel professional should be able to make the necessary arrangements for you.

- Always pack any important medications or supplies you need in your carryon bag so you have easy in-flight access to them
- Try to arrange for an aisle seat so you can more easily communicate with the flight staff
- Be sure to alert the airline of your special needs when you make your flight reservations

- Double check to make sure that the information is on your airline ticket or itinerary
- Ask for wheelchair assistance getting to the gate–it will make it much easier for you to navigate the airport. And you will have someone to guide you to the check-in-counter, security lines, and get you to the proper departure gate.
- Show up early so you start your adventure relaxed. (See our chapter on Accessible Air Travel).

A simple trick when traveling is to use raised stick-on-dots to help you identify your luggage, hotel room, your floor on the elevator panel, etc. If you haven't used them, give it a try. You'll be surprised how well they work.

THE ADVANTAGES OF CRUISING
A cruise is probably the best vacation choice for the visually impaired.
- Cruise ships can provide service packages to help you navigate around the ship
- Elevators and public area signage are in Braille
- Crews onboard can be very helpful, as well
- Cruise ships will provide orientation tours so you can become familiar with your surroundings
- You can request qualified readers to assist you while onboard
- All cruise lines will provide you with a special needs form so you can alert them ahead of time to your specific requirements
- Typically cruise lines offer large print menus and daily newsletters

When you take a cruise
- You unpack once and then enjoy each port
- You can book your off-ship excursions before you sail or while you are on board
- You can take your trips with a group so you are not on your own

Land tours may be a bit more difficult. Tour groups tend to frown on anyone who slows the group down or needs extra attention. If you plan to include land tours on your trip make sure you find a group trip that is designed for special needs travelers. Their pace is slower and they are prepared to give you extra assistance.

TRAVELING WITH A SERVICE DOG
Cruise ships permit service dogs in all public areas, including dining rooms. However, for health reasons your dog will not be permitted in pools, whirlpools or spas. Your service animal must be on a leash, harness or restraining device at all times. Onboard relief areas are also provided for your dog.

If you travel by plane request the bulkhead seat when booking your flight. That will give your dog more room to stretch out

Care and supervision of your dog is your responsibility. The ships are not required to provide food or care for the dog. If you disembark from the ship and leave the animal behind, the crew will not care for your dog.

Be aware that some island states have strict anti-rabies laws which restrict the entrance of all animals, including service animals. Some countries have severe regulations and prolonged quarantines—including the State of Hawaii, Australia, New Zealand, Ireland and the United Kingdom. Be sure to check the regulations for each country you plan to visit.

A Handbook for Special Needs Travelers

This information can be obtained from consulates, or sometimes from the airline you are using. A trained travel professional can help you plan for any contingencies.

If you travel with a service animal you will need documentation of the special status of your animal, as well as the veterinary health certifications required by the countries you plan to visit.

The leather-covered harness, leash, and collar of guide dogs may be made of stainless steel and which will activate the metal detector when your dog goes through the airport security check. If this happens, an airport employee will hold the dog while you go through the metal detector, or you and the dog will be checked by a hand-operated detector.

Travel is a wonderful way to escape the daily routine and get refreshed. Don't sit home and miss all the wonders out there.

START PACKING AND GET GOING!!!

TRAVELING WITH
ℰ AN OLDER PERSON ℐ

Multi-generational travel is more popular today than ever. Nothing is better than families traveling together, creating new memories and sharing that very special family warmth.

But, traveling with an older adult can be more complicated. Preparing for an ordinary trip can be difficult enough, but there are many additional factors to consider when you travel with an older person.

The secret is in the planning. The difficulties an older person faces on a daily basis must be factored into all your planning details. They won't go away on the trip and must be taken into consideration.

First of all, you need to make a list of each potential difficulty and how you plan to handle it. Even issues that seem small at home can become a big deal when you're traveling. Planning ahead can make the difference between a great family trip and a spoiled one. In fact, once the planning is done future trips will be a breeze.

Many families use a trained travel professional with expertise in senior and special needs travel to help avoid any pitfalls. Booking your trip on the internet will not give you any guidance and you could be missing some very important safety and care considerations.

MEDICATIONS

Be sure you take enough medication for your entire trip—with a little extra just in case something unexpected occurs. Make sure you understand the side effects of each medication. Are there certain foods that may not interact well? Do the medications need to be taken at meal times or any other specific times of the day? Do they need to be taken daily? Read and learn all you can before you travel.

EQIPMENT

If special equipment is needed, such as a wheelchair, hospital bed, commode, or oxygen, there are several ways to handle that. You can bring your own, rent it or ship it. If you bring your own, make sure it is in good working order and that you have spare parts for any needed repairs while traveling. Be sure to check all air, bus, or train rule regarding your equipment. (See the chapter on Air Travel With A Disability).

An easier route is to rent whatever equipment you need and have it delivered to your destination. Then you can just use it while on vacation and leave it for pickup by the rentalcompany. But remember you will still be responsible if you need to make repairs while you travel.

CAREGIVING WHILE TRAVELING

If you are a caregiver, try and plan for breaks from your day-to-day caregiving responsibilities. Depending on your budget, family members can all contribute to the cost, not unduly burdening any one family member.

If you are not a caregiver you might want to hire a professional aide to accompany your loved one. Bringing an aide along allows everyone to enjoy their vacation while knowing that all your loved one's needs are properly taken care of.

THE IMPORTANCE OF TRAVEL INSURANCE

Travel insurance is a very important part of your vacation planning. Medicare does not cover your loved one outside the United States, US Virgin Islands and Puerto Rico. It is very important to have the proper coverage for pre-existing health conditions and medical evacuation home should it be necessary. Most of all, should the trip have to be cancelled, you will not lose all your money. (See the chapter on Why Do I Need Travel Insurance? for further details).

TAKING A FAMILY CRUISE

The best multi-generational vacation is a cruise. There are many activities to choose from and there is always something of interest for all age groups. For example, younger family members might want to take an excursion, while older family members might take a ride around town and return to the ship for a nap. Or you might want to take advantage of the many onboard activities that everyone can appreciate. Then you can all meet for dinner and share the day's experiences and enjoy the nighttime shipboard entertainment.

Whatever type of vacation you plan, make sure the pace fits your elder's capabilities. Don't try to fit so much into a day that they end up exhausted and the trip becomes a disaster. Slow down—you might just experience things you would have missed.

Now that you have planned everything and everyone is excited, go out and have a great time making memories that the entire family will cherish forever.

AIR TRAVEL
❦WITH A DISABILITY ❧

In any travel situation the most important things you do are the things you do before you travel.

Whether you're traveling alone, with children, or with a disability—preparation is key. Careful preparation can mean the difference between a successful trip and a stressful, disappointing trip.

And preparation begins with a list. A checklist list of all the things you'll need to do beforehand. Passport (if required), check. Visas (if required), check. Appropriate clothing, check. You get the point. When you're travelling with a disability the only difference is that you need to do a little more preparation. Your check list is a little longer.

Airlines suggest that you arrive at the airport two hours before your flight for security check-in. If you have a disability you should add an additional hour on to that. You've made all your arrangements, but now you need to double check everything. If there is a problem you will have plenty of time to solve it without unnecessary and unwanted stress.

Armed with a few hints and some important information you will know what to expect when you travel.

First, the good news. Since 1986 the federal Air Carrier Access Act of 1986 (ACAA), which affects all aspects of air travel, has helped to assist passengers with disabilities. The act contains more important provisions designed to make air travel safer and easier for the disabled.

The ACAA affects all domestic air carriers, foreign carriers that provide flights to and from the United States, and all airport facilities within the United States and its territories, possessions, and commonwealths. Any new and renovated terminals in the United States must be designed to be accessible to people with disabilities.

All US carriers must follow the regulations, but it is not the same for foreign carriers. For them, the rules apply only to flights that begin or end at US airports and aircraft used for those flights.

Under the act, each airline must provide a Complaint Resolution Officer to be available 24 hours a day to help you solve any flight issues that might arise. Instead of getting angry, frustrated and stressed by an airline employee, you can just ask for their Complaint Resolution Officer. They are your advocates and they are especially trained to help you. If they cannot meet with you in person, they will definitely help you by phone.

A medical certificate is not required except if you are traveling on a stretcher or in an incubator; you will need medical oxygen during a flight; or your medical condition causes reasonable doubt that you can complete the flight without requiring extraordinary medical assistance.

It is always a good idea to notify your airline at least 48 hours in advance of any special needs or requirements you may have.

- Do you need assistance getting from the curb to the plane?
- Are you planning to bring your own oxygen or wheelchair on board?

- Are you bringing a service animal?
- Do you have severe vision or hearing impairments?

Anything out of the ordinary needs to be reported ahead of time. If you do not notify the airline they will try to accommodate, but they cannot delay the flight, and you may end up needing to reschedule your trip.

Simple preparation can save you from a lot of trouble and anxiety.
   When should you book your ticket? As early as you can. It may be difficult for the airline to fill last minute special requests.
   Will you need an oxygen concentrator on board? Check with Advanced Aeromedical (1-800-346-3556) for a complete list of approved oxygen concentrators. If your device is not approved it will not be allowed on the plane.
   Will you need a specific kind of seat when you travel? If you require a specific type of seat, you must make your request at least 24 hours before flight time. However, it is best to do this at the same time you book your ticket to be sure of availability.
   Will you be traveling with medical equipment? Pack all your medical equipment in one suitcase and label it Medical Equipment. The airline will not charge you for baggage packed and labeled in this way. If you put anything else in that bag you must pay the fee.
   Will you be traveling with medications? If you are traveling with medications, make sure they are clearly labeled. This is helpful going through the security checkpoints and if you should need medical attention at your destination.
   Will you need lavatory access? Aircraft with more than one aisle are required to have one accessible lavatory. If the plane has one aisle it may have an accessible lavatory, but it is not required, so you need to ask.
   Will you need to stow your wheelchair? Aircraft that seat 100 or more passengers must provide space to stow at least one typical adult-size manual wheelchair. If that space already has a wheelchair then you must be prepared to stow yours in the cargo hold.

When you stow your wheelchair, take all the removable parts with you on board the aircraft. That way you can avoid the possibility of any parts ending up lost. It is also a good idea to label each removable part for easier reassembly. Attach instructions for assembling the wheelchair so it cannot be removed and easily seen by the crew. Also attach your name, cell phone number and email address. For security reasons, never include your address. All this may seem like a lot of bother, but you only have to do it once and it is well worth the trouble. A very special tip is to shrink wrap your wheelchair so it can go into the cargo hold with all parts attached and none can be lost. Just use plastic wrap to seal everything. It doesn't matter if it is an electric wheelchair or a scooter. Take additional plastic wrap with you for the return flight.

It is always a good idea to bring any articles you will absolutely need on board with you. That way a lost medicine or wheelchair part or article of clothing won't ruin your trip.

If by some chance your wheelchair does get broken call the Global Repair Group (1-877-852-1576) or airlineservices@globalrepairgroup.com. They will come out to the airport and repair your wheelchair.

Special assistance is available for all passengers traveling with a disability. Pre-boarding must be offered to passengers with disabilities. If you have identified yourself at the gate as needing extra time or assistance to board, stow accessibility equipment, or be seated, the airline will accommodate you.

When you land at your destination, you will be the last to deplane. This allows the other passengers to deplane and take their belongings off, leaving you with more room and time to maneuver the aisle.

Need help getting to your seat? Be sure to ask for an aisle chair. The crew will help you into the aisle chair and help you into your seat. When you make your reservation be sure that you ask for an aisle seat with an armrest that lifts up for easy transferring from your aisle chair to your seat.

Want to avoid security screening? Sorry, you can't. No one can. People with disabilities are subject to the same TSA security screening provisions as all other passengers. Security personnel are allowed to examine any assistive devices they believe may conceal a weapon or other prohibited items. However, you may request a private screening, if necessary.

ON BOARD THE AIRCRAFT

Once you're on board, you should be aware of the special in-flight services you can request.

Flight personnel must:

Help you move to and from you seat while getting on and off the aircraft.

Help you prepare for eating. This may include opening your food packages, for example. Personnel are not required to help you eat.

Use an aisle chair to help move you to and from the lavatory. Personnel do not have to help once you are inside the lavatory.

Assist a semi-ambulatory person to move to and from the lavatory. This does not involve lifting or carrying the person.

Store and retrieve your carry-on luggage. Thanks to the Air Carrier Access Act and the cooperation of airlines, traveling with a disability is easier than ever. But it's certainly not perfect. You need to be armed with as much knowledge as possible.

Know your rights.

Know what you need to do to ensure your rights.

Do not be afraid to ask for help.

Do not be intimidated.

You have every right to travel in safety and comfort. If the airline does not comply the Compliance Resolution Officer is your advocate.

A new popular service that makes travel a luxury is "baggage forwarding". This allows you to save time at the airport by avoiding long check-in lines and skipping the wait at the baggage carousel. Pickup and delivery can be done at your hotel, cruise ship, or vacation home, virtually anywhere in the world. It eliminates carrying heavy, bulk luggage and/or sports equipment. For the extra money it gives you total travel convenience.

There's no better time for you to get out there and see the world. You can take that special trip you've always dreamed of. Visit relatives you haven't seen for a while. Join friends on a travel adventure.

Just get out there and enjoy the world.

♋ ACCESSIBLE BUS TRAVEL ♌

In the United States, The Greyhound Line has the most extensive routes and one of the best programs for accommodating special needs travelers.

PREPARATION

Plan early, as with any travel, but at least 48 hours before departure, contact Greyhound's Customers with Disabilities Assist Line at 800-752-4841, to arrange for the assistance you need.

TRAVELING WITH A PERSONAL CARE ATTENDANT

A personal care attendant may travel with you at no additional charge. A ticket will be issued to the attendant only at the time of travel and they are one way only. If you require a return ticket, you must arrange for one at the departure location on the day of travel. If an adult attendant is traveling at no additional charge with a minor that has a disability, the minor will be charged a full adult fare.

TRAVELING WITH A SERVICE ANIMAL

Service animals are allowed to travel with you with proper documentation and vaccinations. They must ride in the coach within your space and may not sit or stand in the aisle of the coach or occupy a seat.

SPECIAL SEATING FOR SPECIAL NEEDS

The front seats on either side of the coach are designated as priority seating for those with special needs. If these seats are taken, the bus driver will ask the seated customer to move to another seat. However, if the request is refused, Greyhound personnel cannot displace the seated customer. If this happens, you will be seated as close to the front as possible and moved forward as seats become available.

TRAVELING WITH CRUTCHES, WALKERS AND WHEELCHAIRS

Crutches, walkers and wheelchairs are allowed inside the coach when they can be stowed safely in the overhead luggage compartment. Power chairs and scooters will be checked as baggage and stowed in the baggage compartment. If you travel with a power chair, be sure to check with the Customers with Disabilities Assist Office for size, weight and other limitations.

Greyhound does have wheelchair lift-equipped buses in its fleet, but you need to check beforehand to be sure on is available on your travel route. With 48 hours advance notice, if one is not available, alternative boarding assistance, such as the Scalamobil or Aislemaster, will be provided. As a last resort you can be lifted manually by Greyhound personnel using the two-person fireman's lift technique, but only if you do not weigh more than 220 pounds.

TRAVELING ABROAD BY BUS

Traveling in Europe by bus is more difficult. There are not as many buses with lifts and they are hard to find. When you make your reservations, check with your tour company, cruise line or travel professional to plan ahead so you are not disappointed when you attempt to travel around.

✄ ACCESSIBLE TRAIN TRAVEL ✄

Amtrak is the major avenue for train travel in the United States and they have made great efforts to accommodate those with special needs.

Make reservations early! If you need accessible bedroom accommodations, a transfer seat or wheelchair space, these are only held for special needs folks up to 14 days before departure. After that they are released to the public. Although Amtrak does not do reserved seating, they will do their best to accommodate requests for seating near an accessible bathroom and lower-level seating in bi-level rail cars. But it's all in the timing – so reserve early.

Amtrak offers a 15% discount for passengers with disabilities and their companion. You are required to provide documentation of your disability at the ticket counter and when boarding the train. This could be a transit system identification card, a membership card from a disability organization or a letter from your doctor. Book your reservations by calling 1-800-USA-RAIL 1-800-872-7245) or in person at a staffed station in order to receive the discount.

Most Amtrak stations are accessible, but don't assume anything. Call Amtrak and double check. The last thing you need is to arrive at the station and discover that you can't get on the train. If you will need assistance, make that request when you make your reservation. Most staffed stations have wheelchairs and wheelchair lifts available. Amtrak employees can also help you to and from restrooms and with the stairs. Even though you have made any assistance requests ahead of time, arrive at least one hour before departure time. At holiday times when the stations are their busiest, give yourself even more time to avoid extra stress.

Reserve early if you want an accessible bedroom! Amtrak trains have at least one coach car with reserved accessible seating and an accessible restroom. Overnight trains offer at least one accessible bedroom in each sleeping car. Accessible seating has space for your wheelchair, a transfer seat and storage for the wheelchair.

Oxygen transport is allowed for passengers if it is required as a medical necessity. You must notify Amtrak of this at least 12 hours in advance of the train's boarding time.

Properly documented and trained service animals are allowed to accompany passengers with disabilities in all customer areas in Amtrak stations, onboard trains and Amtrak Thruway motor coaches.

If service is disrupted for any reason, Amtrak will provide alternate accessible accommodations via motor coach or other transportation.

Meal service is available in room or at seat service on all trains with meal service.

EUROPEAN TRAIN TRAVEL

When traveling in Europe, Rail Europe special amenities for disabled travelers are offered on trains and at many train stations. These are clearly indicated with pictograms, such as toilets and elevators.

Special equipment is available but must be reserved locally in advance. You can do this while in Europe at the train station or through your hotel concierge. Also be sure to specify if you need personal assistance with a wheelchair or boarding, etc.

Generally, European trains are pet friendly, so if you have a service animal it should not be a problem. However, be sure to mention this when you make your reservation.

WHY DO I
❧ NEED TRAVEL INSURANCE? ❧

Proper travel insurance is essential for many reasons. No matter how much you plan for a vacation, things can happen. And who wants to bring unnecessary worries on their vacation?

If you are concerned about medical expenses out of the US, and especially the cost of an emergency evacuation, you absolutely need travel insurance. The cost of an evacuation from the Caribbean might cost $20,000. If you are vacationing in some remote part of the globe it can run upwards of $100,000.

To cover evacuations and pre-existing conditions, you must purchase the policy as soon as possible after you put down your deposit. Preferably within the first 10 days. Cost is based on the age of the traveler and the cost of the trip. In some cases, children traveling with an adult are free. You need to check with your travel professional for details.

Travel insurance also ensures that you will get your money back if you cancel your trip. Depending on the policy, you can be reimbursed if you cancel your trip or come home early because a family member or traveling companion becomes ill. You can also get "cancel for any reason" insurance, but that is more costly. To be sure you are getting the right insurance for you, review the policy carefully.

If you pay using a major credit card, you may be covered for baggage loss, rental car damage, and accidental death or dismemberment. American Express may also cover medical evacuation under certain conditions. Check with your credit card company to make sure which coverage they offer.

Annual travel policies can cover emergency treatment. This is important if your regular coverage or Medigap policy does not cover you outside the US or your home state. If you travel frequently or have a vacation home, annual travel policies may cover medical evacuation for a full year. The right policy can cover medical expenses, evacuation, trip interruption or cancellation, and financial default by your trip provider.

Most travel agencies and tour operators offer travel insurance. Be sure that the policy you are getting comes from a reputable company such as Travel Guard or Travelex. Your travel professional is there to guide you, so be sure all your questions are answered.

It can't be repeated enough: you should always travel with insurance. If anything unforeseen should happen, you may not only lose all your vacation money, but you will have to deal with added stress. And who needs that. It is much better to start your vacation knowing that all your areas of concern are covered.

So you can leave worry at home while you're on vacation.
And travel with peace of mind.

 Linda C. Cutrupi

Linda Carole Cutrupi was born in Bergen County, New Jersey and has continued to reside there. During her career she was the National Conference Manager for the Juvenile Diabetes Foundation International and Leukemia and Lymphoma Society of America, Inc. and in 1988 she formed her own meeting planning company for the purpose of doing medical meeting planning and travel. While planning national and international events, she gained much of her travel experience. In 2002 Linda C. Cutupi formed **Mainly Special Needs Travel**. The inspiration for this came from her mother who had several strokes in 1996 and had no intention of staying home. Linda now uses her expertise to help others.

25339081R00033

Made in the USA
Middletown, DE
30 October 2015